WNBA Hot Ticket

PHOENIX MERCURY

JOSH ANDERSON

Lerner Publications ◆ Minneapolis

To Leo and Dane, the biggest superstars I've ever met.

The stats and information in this book are accurate through August 2024.

Lerner Publications Company
An imprint of Lerner Publishing Group, Inc.
241 First Avenue North
Minneapolis, MN 55401 USA

For reading levels and more information, look up this title at www.lernerbooks.com.

Main body text set in Aptifer Slab LT Pro / Typeface provided by Linotype AG

Library of Congress Cataloging-in-Publication Data

Names: Anderson, Josh, author.
Title: Phoenix Mercury / Josh Anderson.
Description: Minneapolis, MN : Lerner Publications, [2025] | Series: WNBA hot ticket (Lerner sports) | Includes bibliographical references and index. | Audience: Ages 7–11 | Audience: Grades 2–3 | Summary: "The Phoenix Mercury are one of the most successful teams in WNBA history. Read about the players, big plays, and championship seasons that make the Mercury an iconic WNBA franchise"—Provided by publisher.
Identifiers: LCCN 2024030321 (print) | LCCN 2024030322 (ebook) | ISBN 9798765669730 (library binding) | ISBN 9798765670019 (paperback) | ISBN 9798765670033 (epub)
Subjects: LCSH: Phoenix Mercury (Basketball team)—Juvenile literature. | Basketball for women—United States—Juvenile literature. | Women basketball players—United States—Juvenile literature.
Classification: LCC GV885.52.P46 A53 2025 (print) | LCC GV885.52.P46 (ebook) | DDC 796.323640979173—dc23/eng/20240701

LC record available at https://lccn.loc.gov/2024030321
LC ebook record available at https://lccn.loc.gov/2024030322

Manufactured in the United States of America
1 - CG - 12/15/24

TABLE OF CONTENTS

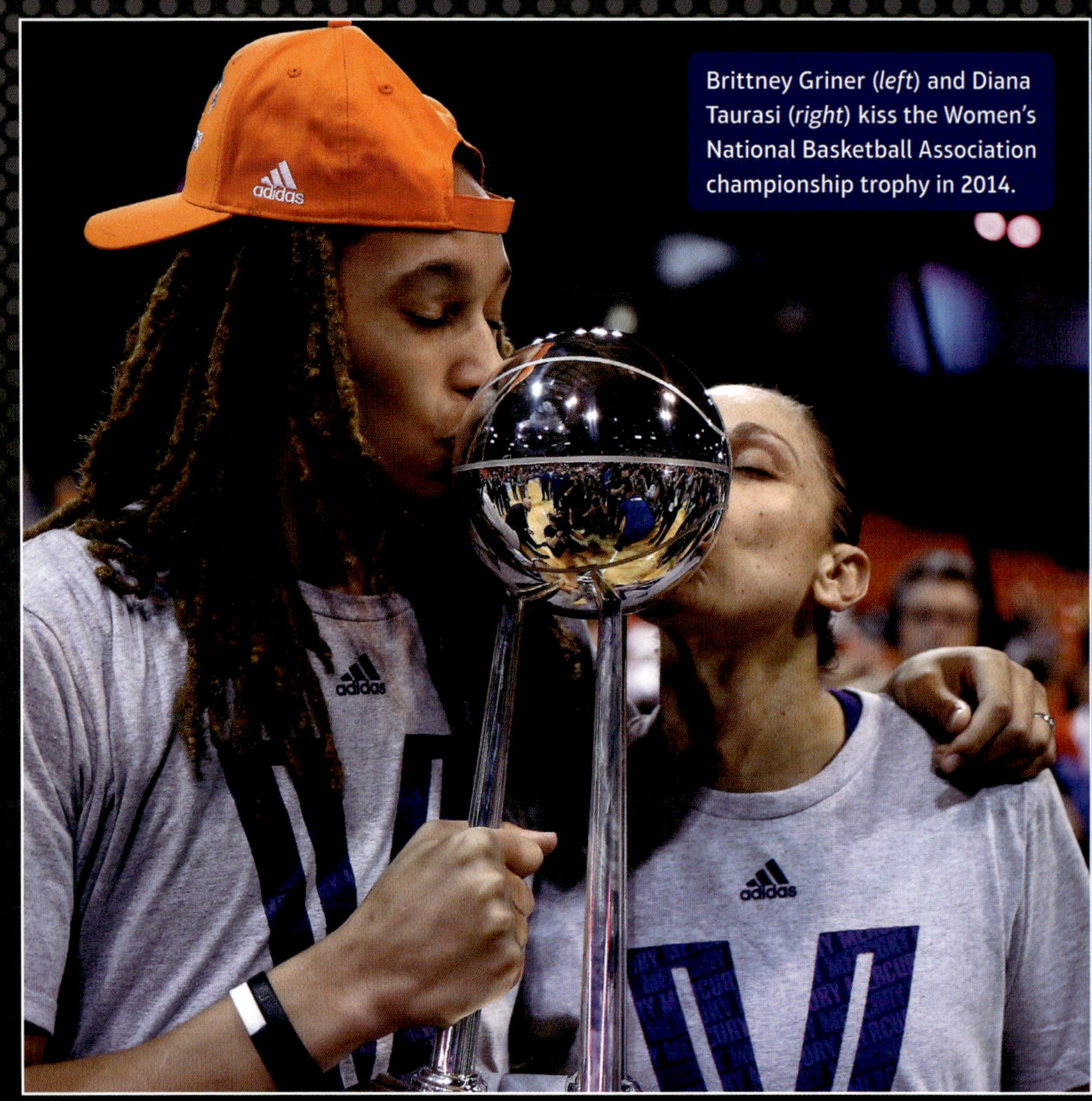

Brittney Griner (*left*) and Diana Taurasi (*right*) kiss the Women's National Basketball Association championship trophy in 2014.

TAURASI'S THIRD TITLE

FACTS AT A GLANCE

- The **PHOENIX MERCURY** defeated the Chicago Sky in the 2014 Women's National Basketball Association (WNBA) Finals to win the team's third league championship.
- Before the 2024 season, the Mercury traded for top scorer **KAHLEAH COPPER**.
- Phoenix chose center **BRITTNEY GRINER** with the first overall pick in the 2013 WNBA Draft.
- Mercury guard **DIANA TAURASI** is the leading scorer in WNBA history.

One basket. That's all superstar Diana Taurasi needed, and the 2014 WNBA championship would belong to the Phoenix Mercury. Taurasi had been here before. In 2007 and 2009, she led Phoenix to the title.

The 2014 WNBA Finals pitted Taurasi's Mercury against the Chicago Sky. The Mercury had won the first two games. The score in Game 3 was tied 82–82. With less than 20 seconds left in the fourth quarter, Taurasi dribbled the ball near the half-court line.

The Sky's Courtney Vandersloot guarded Taurasi, determined not to let her score. With time running down, the other four Mercury players cleared out from the right side of the court. They wanted to give

Taurasi room to go one-on-one against Vandersloot. Taurasi dribbled toward the baseline. With Vandersloot close to her, Taurasi moved to her right as she rose and shot a 16-foot (4.9 m) jump shot.

The ball floated toward the rim as one of the referees blew their whistle. The shot swished through the net, and Vandersloot had fouled Taurasi on the play. Taurasi sank her free throw to give the Mercury an 85–82 lead with 14 seconds left. The Mercury won the game 87–82 and secured their third WNBA title.

The Mercury played in eight straight WNBA playoffs after their 2014 championship. They lost the 2021 WNBA Finals to the Sky. The Mercury's 10-season playoff streak ended in 2023 when they set a team record with 31 losses. After the poor finish, the Mercury traded for one of the league's top scorers, Kahleah Copper. New coach Nate Tibbetts hopes that teaming Copper with WNBA legends Taurasi and Brittney Griner will put the Mercury right back into the playoff picture.

The Mercury present then-president Barack Obama (*left*) with a team jersey at the White House after their 2014 championship win.

Diana Taurasi won the 2014 WNBA Finals Most Valuable Player award after leading her team to their third championship.

Mercury guard Umeki Webb (*left*) drives past a Los Angeles Sparks defender during the 1997 season.

CHAPTER 1

ORIGINAL TEAM

The Mercury were one of the eight original teams to compete in the WNBA's first season in 1997. The team was successful right away. With Women's Basketball Hall of Famers Jennifer Gillom and Michele Timms leading the way, the Mercury reached the WNBA semifinals in the league's first season.

The next season, Phoenix defeated the Cleveland Rockers in the semifinals and faced the Houston Comets in the 1998 WNBA Finals. The Comets won the series in three games. But the Mercury's success helped to create a fan base that would support the team for years to come.

Jennifer Gillom (*center*) shoots over two Houston Comets defenders during the 1998 WNBA Finals.

After winning only eight games during the 2003 WNBA season, the Mercury chose first overall in the 2004 WNBA Draft. The team picked University of Connecticut star Diana Taurasi. The guard immediately became one of the league's top players.

While Phoenix improved as soon as Taurasi joined the team, they did not return to the playoffs until 2007. The 2007 team was led by former National Basketball Association (NBA) championship coach Paul Westhead. He helped the Mercury make it to the Finals that year.

The Mercury fell behind in the series twice to the Detroit Shock. But Phoenix finally won a thrilling five-game victory to give Mercury fans their first WNBA title. After averaging 22 points per game in the series, Phoenix guard Cappie Pondexter was named Finals Most Valuable Player (MVP).

Diana Taurasi is one of only 12 women to win a WNBA championship, a college national championship, a Basketball World Cup, and an Olympic gold medal.

Cappie Pondexter averaged 19.2 points per game when she played for the Mercury from 2006 to 2009.

The Mercury made the Finals again in 2009, winning another thriller in five games against the Indiana Fever. Taurasi averaged more than 20 points and nearly seven rebounds per game. She won the honor of Finals MVP.

When Taurasi spent most of the 2012 season on the bench with an injury, Phoenix had its worst season in team history. They won only

HOOPS SCOOP

The first All-Star in Mercury history was Michele Timms in 1999.

Before joining the Mercury, Kahleah Copper scored 2,677 points in seven seasons with the Chicago Sky.

seven games. As they had in 2004, the Mercury chose first in the 2013 WNBA Draft. They picked another star of college basketball, Baylor University's 6-foot-9 (2.1 m) center Brittney Griner.

Griner and Taurasi helped the Mercury to 10 straight playoff appearances beginning in 2013. They took two more trips to the Finals and won another championship in 2014. After missing the 2023 playoffs, the Mercury traded for Kahleah Copper with an eye on the team's future. The Mercury hope to compete for another championship soon.

AVOIDING TRAGEDY

The Mercury and their NBA neighbors, the Phoenix Suns, are working to end gun violence. By sharing resources on their websites, the teams encourage members of the community to do the same. The websites include links to give money to groups fighting gun violence, including Moms Demand Action and Everytown for Gun Safety. The Mercury also provide links and information to help people vote and to select leaders who share their values.

Taking part in gun-safety groups gives Mercury players a chance to make a difference off the court.

Jennifer Gillom became a member of the Women's Basketball Hall of Fame in 2009.

CHAPTER 2

PHOENIX STARS

Stars Michele Timms and Jennifer Gillom led the Mercury in the team's early years. Timms was a 5-foot-7 (1.7 m) guard who finished in the top six in assists three times during her five seasons in Phoenix. Gillom, a power forward, was the team's leading scorer in each of the Mercury's first three seasons.

Penny Taylor was with Phoenix from 2004 to 2016. The three-time WNBA All-Star is one of only two players to play for the team during all three of its championship seasons. Taylor's career free throw percentage of nearly 87 percent ranks 15th in WNBA history.

Michele Timms drives to the basket during a 2001 game in Miami, Florida.

Although she only stayed in Phoenix for four seasons, guard Cappie Pondexter helped lead the Mercury to two WNBA titles. She was chosen as an All-Star seven times in her career. Pondexter averaged more than 19 points per game during her time in Phoenix and won the 2007 WNBA Finals MVP award.

The winningest coach in team history is Sandy Brondello. She led the Mercury from 2014 to 2021. Brondello won 150 games and coached the Mercury to the playoffs in each of her eight seasons with the team. Brondello led the team to the 2014 WNBA title in her first year as the Phoenix coach.

Sandy Brondello became the head coach of the New York Liberty after eight seasons in Phoenix.

While Phoenix had to give up valuable draft picks in the trade to get Kahleah Copper, the team got a true star. Copper became one of the best scorers in the league during her last three seasons in Chicago. She earned four All-Star selections in a row.

Copper seemed to reach an even higher level when she first arrived in Phoenix in 2024. In her second game for the Mercury, she scored a career-high 38 points in a game against the Atlanta Dream. Then, three nights later, she scored 37 against the Las Vegas Aces. She is only the second player in league history to have back-to-back games with 35 or more points.

Kahleah Copper (*right*) dribbles around Las Vegas Aces defender Jackie Young during a 2024 game.

Brittney Griner is not only one of the tallest players in WNBA history. She is also one of the greatest. Since the Mercury drafted Griner in 2013, she's been an All-Star nine times and won the league's Defensive Player of the Year award twice. Griner has led the league in blocks six times and ranks third all-time in the category.

Diana Taurasi's amazing career started in 2004 and has continued for 20 years. The 11-time All-Star finished in the top 10 in MVP voting 14 times, winning the award in 2009. She helped the Mercury to three WNBA titles. She has scored more than 15 points per game in every season except for two when she was slowed by injury. Taurasi is the WNBA's all-time leader in points and three-point baskets, and she ranks fifth in career assists.

Diana Taurasi (*right*) won three college national championships during her four years at the University of Connecticut.

HOOPS SCOOP

Brittney Griner's 129 blocks in 2014 are the most all-time in a single WNBA season.

Brittney Griner (*leaping in white*) blocks a shot by a Seattle Storm player.

Shey Peddy raises her arms after a Mercury victory. She played with the Washington Mystics before moving to Phoenix during the 2020 season.

CHAPTER 3

INCREDIBLE MOMENTS

The 2020 WNBA season was probably the strangest in league history. To prevent spreading the disease COVID-19, the entire season was played at IMG Academy in Bradenton, Florida. Players were used to competing in front of screaming, cheering fans. But the games at IMG were played in a nearly empty arena.

The Mercury celebrate their Game 1 win over the Washington Mystics during the 2020 playoffs.

Both the season and the playoffs were shortened that year. After a 13–9 finish to the season, the Mercury faced the Washington Mystics in a single-game playoff. The winner would move on, while the losing team's season was over.

With 5.8 seconds left to go in the game and the Mercury down 84–82, it looked like Phoenix would be the team on the losing end. After a timeout, Diana Taurasi passed the ball to teammate Skylar Diggins-Smith. Diggins-Smith drove toward the hoop. She sent a high pass over the defense to Shey Peddy standing in the corner behind the three-point line. Peddy faked a shot and her defender leaped, trying for the block.

Skylar Diggins-Smith dribbles toward the basket during the 2020 WNBA playoffs.

Shey Peddy attempted four three-pointers during the first game of the 2020 playoffs. She made two of them, including the shot that won the game against Washington.

After her defender was past her, Peddy jumped and sank a three-pointer with no time left to give Phoenix the dramatic 85–84 win. Peddy never played in an All-Star Game or scored more than 10 points per game in a season. But that night, she gave Mercury fans a memory that would last for a lifetime.

HOOPS SCOOP

Former Mercury player Cappie Pondexter ranks seventh on the WNBA all-time scoring list with 6,811 points.

Brittney Griner averaged 17.6 points and 7.5 rebounds per game in her first 10 seasons with the Mercury.

WNBA fans knew to expect the unexpected when Brittney Griner came into the league in 2013. In her first game, she gave them a preview of her incredible career to come. She became the first player in WNBA history to make a slam dunk twice in one game.

Since her first season in 2004, Diana Taurasi has finished in the top 10 in scoring 14 times. But it wasn't until 2017 that she was able to call herself the greatest scorer in league history. On June 18, with basketball legend Kobe Bryant watching from the crowd, Taurasi scored her 7,489th WNBA point. She passed Tina Thompson and became the league's all-time scoring leader. Taurasi has scored more than 10,000 points in her career. While any record can be broken, it's hard to imagine that Taurasi's will not last for quite some time.

Many consider Diana Taurasi to be the best point guard ever to play basketball.

Kahleah Copper (*right*) shoots over Dallas Wings defender Natasha Howard during a 2024 game.

CHAPTER 4

HOT AS THE DESERT SUN

After years of trailing far behind men's basketball in popularity, women's hoops and the WNBA are on the rise. After shrinking from a high of 16 teams in the early 2000s down to 12, the league will expand for the first time in over a decade in 2025. One new team, the Valkyries, will play in Northern California in the same arena as the NBA's Golden State Warriors. Another team will begin play in Toronto, Ontario, Canada, in 2026.

Brittney Griner (*left*) and Diana Taurasi (*right*) are part of the USA Basketball Olympic team. Griner has won three gold medals, and Taurasi has won six.

At some point in the future, the Mercury will have a roster that doesn't include Diana Taurasi and Brittney Griner. They are two of the best to ever play the game of basketball. How will the team respond?

When the Mercury hired Nate Tibbetts ahead of the 2024 season, he became the highest-paid coach in WNBA history. Beyond his two future Hall of Famers, Tibbetts has plenty of talent on the roster to get the Mercury back into the playoff picture. Copper began her Mercury career by showing that she can keep pace with the best talents in the league. Guard Sophie Cunningham provides shooting and rebounding for the team. The Mercury have been at the top of the WNBA since 2014. Fans hope Tibbetts can keep them there for a long time to come.

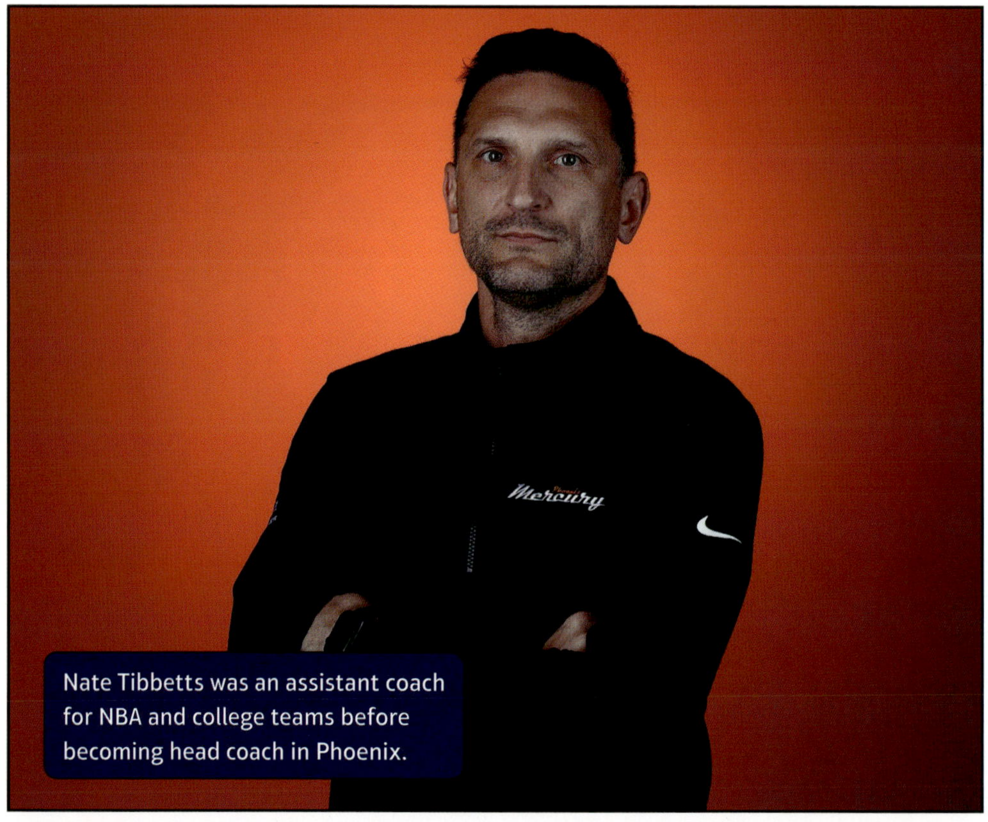

Nate Tibbetts was an assistant coach for NBA and college teams before becoming head coach in Phoenix.

Sophie Cunningham joined the Mercury in 2019 after a successful college basketball career at the University of Missouri.

GLOSSARY

All-Star: one of the best players in a sports league. Each season, WNBA All-Stars play in the All-Star Game.

assist: a pass that leads directly to a basket

baseline: the line that runs along the court behind each basket

block: when the ball is knocked away by a defender before reaching the hoop

draft: an event in which teams take turns choosing new players

free throw: an open shot taken from behind a set line after a foul by an opponent

jump shot: a shot in basketball made by jumping into the air and releasing the ball with one or both hands at the peak of the jump

rebound: grabbing and controlling the ball after a missed shot

roster: a list of players on a team

semifinal: a game or a series of games coming before the final round in a tournament

slam dunk: a shot in basketball made by jumping high into the air and throwing the ball down through the basket

title: championship

Women's Basketball Hall of Fame: a museum in Knoxville, Tennessee, that honors the best women to play or coach basketball

LEARN MORE

Diana Taurasi
http://dianataurasi.com/

Lowe, Alexander. *G.O.A.T. Basketball Point Guards*. Minneapolis: Lerner Publications, 2023.

Phoenix Mercury
https://mercury.wnba.com/

Rajczak Nelson, Kristen. *Diana Taurasi: Basketball GOAT.* Buffalo, NY: Gareth Stevens Publishing, 2024.

Whiting, Jim. *The Story of the Phoenix Mercury*. Mankato, MN: Creative Education and Creative Paperbacks, 2024.

WNBA
https://www.wnba.com/

INDEX

PHOTO ACKNOWLEDGMENTS

Image credits: Image credits: Jonathan Daniel/Getty Images Sport/Getty Images, p.4; Oliver Douliery/Getty Images News/Getty Images, p.6; Jonathan Daniel/Getty Images Sport/Getty Images, p.7; Harry How/Allsport/Getty Images, p.8; Todd Warshaw/Allsport/Getty Images, p. 9; Gregory Shamus/Getty Images Sport/Getty Images, p.10; Christian Petersen/Getty Images Sport/Getty Images, p.11; Cooper Neill/Getty Images Sport/Getty Images, p.12; Craig Jones/Allsport/Getty Images, p.13; Otto Greule Jr./Allsport/Getty Images, p.14; Scott Troyanos/Allsport/Getty Images, p.15; Quinn Harris/Icon Sportswire/Getty Images, p.16; Ethan Miller/Getty Images Sport/Getty Images, p.17; Christian Petersen/Getty Images Sport/Getty Images, p.18; Steph Chambers/Getty Images Sport/Getty Images, p.19; Julio Aguilar/Getty Images Sport/Getty Images, p.20; Julio Aguilar/Getty Images Sport/Getty Images, p.21; Julio Aguilar/Getty Images Sport/Getty Images, p.22; Julio Aguilar/Icon Sportswire/Getty Images, p.23; Christian Petersen/Getty Images Sport/Getty Images, p.24; Chris Coduto/Getty Images Sport/Getty Images, p.25; Cooper Neill/Getty Images Sport/Getty Images, p.26; Dustin Satloff/Getty Images Sport/Getty Images, p.27; Christian Petersen/Getty Images Sport/Getty Images, p.28; M. Anthony Nesmith/Icon Sportswire/Getty Images, p. 29

Cover image: Ethan Miller/Getty Images Sport/Getty Images